a fo

Brand
for Authors

Creating a Solid Author
Brand for Busy *Writers*

Jenny Kate

This publication is designed to provide accurate and authoritative information in regard to the subject matter covered. It is sold with the understanding that the publisher and author are not engaged in rendering legal, accounting, or other professional services. If legal or other expert assistance is required, the services of a competent professional should be sought.

Copyright © 2024 Jenny Kate

All rights reserved. No part of this book may be reproduced in any form or by any electronic or mechanical means, including information storage and retrieval systems, without permission in writing from the publisher, except by reviewers, who may quote brief passages in a review.

ISBN (print): 978-1-7333961-7-2

ISBN (ebook): 978-1-7333-961-6-5

Editing by Sandra Wendel, Write On, Inc.
Cover by Ronnie Walter
Interior design by Siva Ram Maganti

Published by Mustard Couch Press, a subsidiary of TJC Enterprises, LLC, 2308 Mt Vernon Ave #440, Alexandria, VA 22301

Web: www.thewriternation.com
Instagram: @writernationjen
Facebook.com/WriterNation
Facebook.com/groups/WriterNation
Email: writernationjen@gmail.com

For Miss Thing

Contents

Introduction	vii
Why Listen to Me?	x
What Could You Possibly Get Here You Can't Get Elsewhere?	xi
What Is a Brand?	1
Define Your Brand	2
Why Is an Author Brand Important?	4
Define Your Goals	9
Personal Author Goals	11
Business Goals as an Author	12
Your "Only" Statement	14
Nuts and Bolts	19
Mine from Your Life	20
Mine from Your Books	23
Putting It All Together	25
What Do I Do with My Brand?	28
Author Bios	28
Logos	34
Fonts, Imagery, and Tone	35
Market Your Brand	42
Create Compelling Content	43
Web Presence	45

Print Products	49
Bonus Material	**52**
Bonus #1: Your Author Brand Checklist	53
Acknowledgments	**55**
About the Author	**56**

Introduction

𝓑efore we get started, let's do an exercise in recognition. When you think of Apple (the company), what do you think of? Modern technology, the iPhone, its recognizable logo?

When you think about McDonald's, what comes to mind? Ronald, fun, cheap food, the arches?

What about Jeep? Rugged, outdoors, strength.

Now think about authors.

What immediately comes to mind when you see a new David Baldacci book? Excitement, thriller, great characters.

How about R. L. Stine? Fun, adventurous, scary, for kids.

Toni Morrison? Passionate stories about the African American experience.

Danielle Steel? Romance, sultry, sexy.

The point is when you think about each of these iconic brands, the substance that comes to mind first is not the logo or the colors, but the experience you'll have with each one.

Experience is lasting.

Maya Angelou said, "I've learned that people will forget what you said. People will forget what you did. But people will never forget how you made them feel."

That is the essence of brand. Your personal brand and your professional brand.

How do people feel when they meet you or read your books? These are not two different brands. They are the same brand. The author is just as important as the books.

Have you ever been told, "Don't meet your heroes, they'll disappoint you?" In today's business world—small business, author-owned business, all business—the personality brand of the owner is just as powerful as the product itself.

One of the best marketers in the United States is Seth Godin. He teaches that a brand is a set of expectations, memories, stories, and relationships that, when taken together, account for a customer's decision to choose one product or service over another.

But before we get into what your brand is and how to build it, let's look at a little history.

Have you heard the term *author platform* bounced around the publishing world? It's a terrible way to describe how an author markets their work. The fiction world tried to utilize the term, which works for nonfiction authors, to explain to fiction authors how to build a brand. But platform works way better for nonfiction authors in terms of having a clear, concise, definitive way to market work. A nonfiction author typically writes about a topic they are an expert in. That topic is the platform. That topic is what the nonfiction author is known for.

Most nonfiction authors are solving a problem for the reader. Want to learn how to invest and create wealth? Then there is a book to learn that. How about managing a tough family relationship? Plenty of books on that. Want to become a vegan? Check out the cookbook section of Barnes & Noble. The authors of those books have a platform, a topic of expertise to share with the world.

Trying to equate that to a fiction writer is so confusing that most authors give up trying. Fiction authors' main goal is not to educate a reader. It's to entertain. To tell a story. Sure, there may be elements of education, and you certainly may learn something new, but the main objective of that fiction book is to entertain you, not teach you. So there is no platform to speak of.

Oh, we've tried.

- Your platform is your social media following. Nope. That's influence.
- Your platform is all your books. No. Those are your products.
- Platform is your covers. Your font. Your logo. No, those are marketing tools.

A platform in the sense of an author business is not social media content or blogs or imagery. It's content and expertise. But even then, if you are in fact a nonfiction author, how do you market that content? And if you're a fiction author, what do you even do at all? That's where brand comes in.

An author's brand is the actual experience an author gives to a reader. It's the feeling, the emotion, the adventure an author promises to their reader. When you read a Stephen King book, you know you are about to be scared to death. When you read a Stephen Hawking book, you know you are about to learn something incomprehensible. Maya Angelou? Poetry you feel in your bones. Diana Gabaldon will make you weak in the knees in Scotland. Michael and Jeff Shaara will teach you about the

American Civil War.

While platform is unique to nonfiction authors, brand applies to both a nonfiction author and a fiction author.

Why Listen to Me?

For the same reason I asked you to read my other books on marketing. I've spent my entire career in marketing and communications, and I care about your success. I want you to have the skills to market your books without wanting to die doing it. I wrote this book because I want to help writers feel less overwhelmed, and I have years of experience and education to back it up.

I'm pretty proud of my previous books (I have a list of them at the end of this book) that help you do the same—market your work—and I am honored with reviews like these:

> *"[Jenny] breaks everything down into very small steps. When I was always intimidated and overwhelmed with the idea of marketing my own books, I consider every one of her small steps, and I find myself thinking: I can do this!"* — Marion

> *"A real gold mine! As a new author set to launch in January, this book has been invaluable. Well-written, concise and packed with valuable and practical information for new and already published authors. I have no doubt that I will be reading it several more times."* — Kyle

> *"What I've needed for a very long time."* — Carole

> *"Excellent reference and guide. If you've been beating your head against the wall attempting to fine-tune your marketing strategy, don't despair. Step back and read this book!"* — Nick

> *"Thanks for making something often overwhelming into something manageable, and dare I say, maybe even fun!"* — Becky

Reviews like this are why I founded Writer Nation in 2017 in the first place—to specifically help writers market their work. How that is done foundationally is the same now as it was ten years ago. Your brand still offers an experience. The tactics to do that change from time to time, but the essence of your brand should not. With more than twenty years' experience, I have researched, tried, and tested just about every marketing technique out there, and I can tell you when to try something and when not to bother.

For instance, would I try TikTok right now? Yes, I would. It's the hottest thing and it is selling books. That's the bottom line. But do all writers need to be on TikTok? No. No they don't. Especially if it doesn't match your brand.

If it matters, I'm also a writer, just like you. I wrote my first book in the second grade, collaborated on my first novel in the seventh grade, published my first poem in college and my first short story in 2003. I am currently writing my first commercial fiction series.

What Could You Possibly Get Here You Can't Get Elsewhere?

As with just about any marketing book available to you, most of what you'll find in this book is already all over the internet. There really aren't that many new ideas under the sun, and while marketing on the internet changes all the time, the concepts of brand and marketing do not change.

That being said, do you have hours to comb through all that and figure out what really works? I know you'd rather be writing. So I routinely dig through the mountain of data, test my own ideas, and apply what I find to my own business and help authors. I did the same to design this book.

This book helps you understand your own author brand and how to apply that brand to your work. Having a solid, consistent brand will help you sell books. It will help you increase your followers, find readers, and grow your email list.

As you read the book, keep the following principles in mind:

- **You must take the time to brainstorm your brand.** Do not post a single piece of content until you have fully fleshed out your brand. Who you are to a reader is important. Who you think you are is also important. Understanding both of these concepts will help you build all your content from now on.

- **You must understand your own goals.** What exactly is it you want to achieve in your author career? Don't hold back. If it's to write a *New York Times* best-seller, then own that. If it's to write stories as they come to you, upload them to Amazon, and be okay with modest sales? Own that too. Or maybe it's somewhere in between. Own it. Because your brand needs to reflect your goals. Your goal drives all your marketing.

- **Your brand is your public persona.** Who do you want to be to your reader? This is where privacy also comes in. Maybe you're an open book and it doesn't matter to you, but maybe you're using a pen name. Either way, brands are effective when they are honed and deliberate.

- **You must define your reader.** As much as we'd like to think every person wants to read our book, that's just not the case. Your reader is someone special and that target reader needs to be the person you are talking to and writing for.

I've divided the book into five chapters:

Chapter 1 is the foundation for every other section. It defines exactly what brand means to you.

Chapter 2 covers your author goals. Without a goal, you have no business marketing a book. You are now a small business owner with goals and everything you do is to drive toward that goal.

Chapter 3 discusses how to develop your public persona. This is the essence of your brand. Who are you and what are you offering?

Chapter 4 explains the part of brand most people understand: what it looks like. From font to colors to your author bio, this is where the brand comes to life.

Chapter 5 explains how you project or market your brand.

The final part of this book includes a bonus brand checklist and a bonus press release template. Use the checklist to help you brainstorm everything you've learned in the book.

My last piece of advice is this: Ask for help anytime. Whether you're just starting out and need some advice or you've been at this awhile and are stuck, email or message me. Make sure to sign up for my free email that gives monthly tips and keeps you updated on statistics you need to be successful. Think of me as your marketing partner.

Peace & Prose, & Happy Writing!

Jenny Kate

"People relate to people, and if your brand feels like people, they'll relate to you too."

—Laura Busche, author of *Lean Branding: Creating Dynamic Brands to Generate Conversion* and *Powering Content: Building a Nonstop Content Marketing Machine*

What Is a Brand?

You need a brand, but what exactly is a brand? In the introduction, I gave you some examples of brands and told you that brand is an experience. It's how you make your readers feel. It's the story you tell. It is also the public persona you wish to project and the world of your books. That's it.

People buy books from people they know or think they know. That makes you part of the commodity in the business you are building. Yes, *you* the author are part of the package deal.

That aside, the landscape has evolved. Social media have simply changed things for everyone. Everyone can have a personal brand. People are building lives on their personal brand. They are quitting "regular" jobs, developing personal brands, creating content online and affording their lives. Authors must take advantage of this.

Why?

Amazon defines brand as "how a company differentiates itself from its peer brands."

Even if you don't think you already have an online brand, you probably do. Are you on LinkedIn, Instagram, Facebook? If you post content to any platform on the internet, then you already have a personal brand. You must cultivate that brand, because the age-old saying of, "If you don't talk, they will," matters. Cultivating your brand, paying attention to it, and engaging with it tells your readers you are invested. It also allows you to control that brand.

Define Your Brand

Your author brand, fiction or nonfiction, is a concept that plays a crucial role in building and sustaining your business. It is the holistic perception and reputation of you as author and your books as the promise they offer in the minds of your readers. These eleven elements go into defining what brand is:

1. **Experience.** Remember Seth Godin? The experience is your brand and what readers will remember. It connects to reputation.

2. **Reputation.** Your reputation as an author and the reputation of your books as well as the perception of both are tied to your brand. Are you the kind of person readers want to buy books from? Are your books well-written? Do they adhere to genre standards? Do they take a reader on the expected ride and deliver on promises?

3. **Values.** When I talk about the ride your books take a reader on, I'm talking about genre and values. Your brand communicates the values of you the author and of your books. Are they aligned? When a reader looks at your author page or your covers, are the values of your brand evident?

4. **Emotional connection.** Books give readers an emotional ride. No way around it. Don't you love picking up a

thriller and having your heart pound? What about diving into a fantasy world and being awed? That's the emotional connection I'm talking about. I love Dan Brown's The DaVinci Code. Treasure hunts are my favorite and I'll read anything he writes because I know it's fun and adventurous.

5. **Differentiation.** Your brand helps you stand out. I'll help you define this in chapter 3. But if you and your books do not stand out in a crowded market (and believe me, the book market is swamped!), you will not be successful.

6. **Consistency.** Your brand is a consistent brand identity across all aspects of your marketing. Inconsistency confuses readers, and, frankly, in today's world, you cannot afford to confuse anyone. For example, J.K. Rowling had trouble selling adult thrillers because she was so well-known for Harry Potter. That doesn't mean you can't write in multiple genres, but you do need to be aware that doing so could confuse your readers. You might consider a pen name to distinguish between them.

7. **Long-term value.** Yes, you and your books provide long-term value to a reader. Series are killing it right now, and have been for years, because a good, solid brand brings long-term value to a reader. If readers know the value of your stories, if they know what to expect, they'll stick around as long as you're producing books. Susan Wigg's Lakeshore Chronicles are a good example or David Baldacci's Camel Club thrillers.

8. **Loyalty.** The long-term value of your author brand fosters amazing reader loyalty. And you want that. You want loyal readers who turn into fans. Remember, people buy from brands (read: people) they like, know, and trust. A strong brand generates the kind of loyalty that sustains a lengthy career. How many times do you go straight to an author you already know to see if he or she has a new book out? Stephen King, anyone?

9. **Superfans are your best advocates.** Connected to loyalty is advocacy. Once you turn a reader into a loyal fan, your brand can turn them into a superfan. Your superfans will sell your books for you. They will post glowing reviews and tell their friends and recommend your books to their book club. Spend time nurturing your fans and rewarding superfans with things like secret podcast episodes, character dossiers, alternate endings and beginnings, or additional chapters.

10. **Framework.** A brand is a consistent framework that allows you to convey to your reader exactly what you offer and why they'll love it. This is why you need to take the time to develop the brand. The more time and effort you put into building and understanding your brand, the easier marketing actually becomes.

11. **Identity.** Your brand is the face of your author business.

Why Is an Author Brand Important?

Because analysts assert that more than 2.3 million indie books were self-published in 2021, and *Publishers Weekly* estimates that number will keep going up. By that estimate, 191,000 books are indie-published every month across a multitude of publishing sites such as Kobo and Apple Books, but Amazon takes the lion's share. To make it a bit more palatable, most of those books are one-offs, and the average number of copies sold on one title is 100. So if you're in publishing for the long game, that monthly number shouldn't look quite so daunting.

That being said, traditional publishing houses publish up to one million titles a year. Penguin Random House alone published more than 80,000 titles last year.

In addition, more than 54,000 Americans registered as writers and authors in 2022, according to the Bureau of Labor Statistics, which is 4,000 more than in 2021. Some of this is attributed to the changes in the industry that makes self-publishing, or indie publishing, easier. The barriers to entry into indie publishing are largely gone.

I don't tell you these statistics to scare you off or deter you from publishing. I tell you so you'll understand that you absolutely need to find a way to stand out. If you want to make a career out of writing, you must have a business plan and you must think of yourself as a business.

The first step in that is understanding that author brands are personal brands. Most of those are cultivated online these days. I would argue all of them are cultivated online because of the way Americans run their lives. We're all on our phones. We bank on our phones. We drive using Google maps. We buy things from apps on our phones. And we read on our phones.

According to research firm Statista, 90 percent of the American population uses social media, and 85 percent of Americans use a smartphone. The point is you can't cultivate a brand without the internet. Your personal brand is an author brand. The way to build and grow that personal author brand is through social media. The way to sell books is through advertising and email marketing.

There's no way around the connection of an author brand to a personal brand, and there's no way around the building of that brand anywhere else but online—the most effective way to grow your author business and sell books.

Your author brand sets you apart from the crowd. It provides you a distinct identity online and offline. This unique identity helps readers recognize and remember your work. When they walk into a Barnes & Noble, or flip through Amazon, the overt branding will stand out to them—font, colors, book covers. When they walk into a book signing or author event, they'll know what to expect.

That expectation is designed through recognition and familiarity. Your strong brand creates a sense of comfort and trust because your reader knows what to expect. All of this encourages repeat readership and loyalty. And that's what you're after—a reader who wants to read all of your books or even your only book.

Something else a strong brand offers is that it allows authors to connect with readers on an emotional level. Through shared values and experiences, your brand can resonate with readers, and that creates a stronger bond between you and your reader.

With a consistent brand that readers recognize and are familiar with, you are building trust and credibility. This is really important. If your brand projects one thing and the books another and you the author something entirely different, the reader doesn't know what to expect and mistrust will get in the way of the bond. That bond builds your career.

Make sure your brand gives the reader what you are promising. Have someone, and it doesn't have to be a public relations person, look at your message, image, colors, fonts, values, website, social media accounts, book covers, and book content. Are they all saying the same thing?

Because in addition to building trust and credibility, you are also building visibility and discoverability. In an age dominated by social media and other online platforms, you need to make yourself and your books more searchable, shareable, and more easily found by potential readers.

Standing out in the crowd allows you to define a unique niche, which is essential to every author. How are you different from other authors in your genre? That needs to be defined. Your style differentiates you from other authors. Define that. This is how you attract more readers who are specifically attracted to what you offer. I'll help you do that in the next chapter.

Wrap Up

What is a brand? It is the experience you offer the reader. It encompasses you as the author and the books as the product. A brand is a framework you can use to market your work effectively.

Why do you need a brand? You need a brand to stand out in a saturated market. That's really the bottom line. If you plan to sell books, then you need to show a potential reader why they should take a chance on you. A consistent brand can do that.

"You can't play it safe. In order to create amazing shifts and transformations, you've got to dig in."

—Amy Porterfield, author of *Two Weeks Notice: Find the Courage to Quit Your Job, Make More Money, Work Where You Want, and Change the World*

Define Your Goals

To start building your brand, let's start with some basics. Do you think of your author business as a small business? You should. If you plan to sell books for any reason, then you are absolutely building a business. It is important for you to see this venture as a business, because whether you are planning to publish traditionally or indie, you will be responsible for a large chunk of the enterprise. Really defining and understanding the goals of your business help you develop your brand.

The second basic is goals. Goals are an essential aspect of human life, and they drive productivity. They can provide a sense of direction and purpose. They can also help you understand what you're trying to achieve. Goals are beneficial to your author journey for several reasons.

They give your writing meaning. All that time you spend in

front of the computer has meaning if you understand why you're doing it. In that vein, it can keep impostor syndrome at bay, and what author couldn't stand to keep that monster in a box?

Goals also give you motivation. A clear target—whether it's a complete book or number of words/pages written, or the *New York Times* best-seller list—can inspire you to keep going. It can inspire you to sit at the computer or pick up a pen. Motivation can inspire you to overcome writer's block or impostor syndrome. It can also keep you committed to your desired end result.

Lack of focus? Goals can help you concentrate your efforts on specific tasks and priorities to get the book finished or dive into your marketing. In some ways, goals can prevent distractions. They can help you channel all your energy toward the prize at the end.

How do you feel about measuring success? Some authors hate anything to do with analytics, but some authors live by them. Goals can provide milestones, which in turn give you something to measure progress and tools to adjust to stay on course.

Pursuing goals gives you the opportunity to grow personally and professionally. That pursuit often requires writers to learn new skills (social media ads or podcasting, anyone?) and overcome challenges (frustration and limitations). The incredibly fulfilling process of learning new skills allows you to push your limits and get better.

I'm the worst about time management. But having goals allows me the opportunity to prioritize my time. Efficiency is key to production. How efficient are you at your writing? By allocating your time appropriately, you can reach your goals more efficiently.

Speaking of efficient, goals provide you with a framework to make decisions faster. If you know where you are headed, then evaluating options in front of you becomes easier. You can assess whether the writing or the research or the book signing aligns with your goals and kick to the curb those that don't, resulting in a way more efficient use of your time and energy.

Do you love a good to-do list? I do. I love checking items off that bad boy too. Goals allow me this small thrill in my day. Experts say that a sense of accomplishment, even if it's checking one more item off my goals list, contributes to overall happiness and well-being. Who wouldn't like that?

So what goals are you trying to build? The goals you need to think about are your writing or author goals and your business goals. I'll help you do that next.

Personal Author Goals

This goal is almost always easier than the business goals. Do you want to be a *New York Times* best-seller? Are you good with selling books and making a modest living? What about a *USA Today* best-seller or selling enough books for a car payment?

Sit down and write your author goals.

Maybe you want to publish four books a year. Maybe it's four books a month. Whatever you want to accomplish as a writer needs to be written down where you can see it.

I listen to Joanna Penn's podcast, The Creative Penn, religiously. She had a successful indie author on one week who said something that resonated with me. She said, "I'm happy to be a six-figure author no one has ever heard of."

Well, me too! If I could sustain my life with my writing, and I wasn't a national celebrity author, I'd be a very happy girl. I'd have control over my life, no boss to speak of, no noisy cube farm to work in, no supervisor to fight about telework with. I'd be writing books and publishing books and talking about books. What a life!

So now I want you to think about your author goals. What do you want? What will you be happy with?

Once you know that, then you can start thinking through how to get there. That's where your business goals come in. Your personal author goals are only achieved through your author business goals.

Business Goals as an Author

To achieve your best-seller status or pay your monthly car payment, you need to have some idea of what it takes to make that happen. This section will get a little business wonky, but it's important. Doing all this thinking now only helps you reach your goals later. It is a critical step in your author business. Your business goals provide direction, purpose, and a roadmap for your author growth and success.

So let's get to it. Grab a piece of paper or type this out on your computer, but take advantage of this section and detail for yourself exactly what you need to do.

First, you must understand your vision. Clarify your long-term vision for your author career. This really goes back to your author goal. Where do you want to be in five, ten, or fifteen years?

Second, use SMART goals to help you. It's the gold standard for goal setting. Each goal should include each aspect of the SMART system. Here's a little primer:

- **Specific.** Use strong, specific, clear, precise objectives. Be exact and define what you want to accomplish. How many books do you need to produce and sell to make the amount of money you are expecting to make?
- **Measurable.** Establish concrete criteria for measuring your progress and success. This can include number of books or words or pages or amount of time spent writing. It can also include the number of emails you'll produce, ads you'll create, social content to post.
- **Achievable.** Be realistic. Are your goals attainable? Do you have the resources you need to make that happen?

- **Relevant.** Make sure they make sense for the market. In other words, you wouldn't have a goal to produce one romance a year for a series and expect to compete. Romance series have aggressive timelines.
- **Time-bound.** Give yourself a timeframe for completing your goal. A year for one book? A year to sell four books? A month to write a first draft? Maybe write 2,000 words per day?

Some examples of author business production goals might look like this:

Annual Goals:

- I will write four books in my genre this year.
- I will sell 100 books a month testing three Amazon ads per book, posting on social three days a week, and writing one email a week.
- I will attend two major fiction conferences this year and focus on character development and pacing workshops.

Daily Goals:

- I will write 2,000 words in chapter one before noon today.
- I will produce five pieces of social content for Instagram today.
- I will write a 250-word email and schedule it for sending by 3:00 p.m.

For your actual business goals, you'll want to consider a slew of goals.

- **Financial goals.** What annual or monthly revenue do you plan to bring in? How profitable are your books? Looking at expenses in and expenses out helps develop this goal.
- **Marketing and sales goals.** How many books do you want to launch in a specific period of time? How many books do you want to sell? What marketing tools will you use?

- **Productivity goals.** How much do you want to write? How often? How many books do you want to write and in what period of time? If you're indie publishing, how long do you expect it to take to edit, revise, format, and upload your book?
- **Operational goals.** These goals look at how efficient you are being with your production. Is there a way to improve your efficiency or reduce your cost of publishing?
- **Professional growth goals.** How are you going to improve your craft? Whether its conferences, workshops, online courses, define how you will improve your products.

Create a goal sheet with milestones to meet those goals. Those milestones keep you motivated and on track.

For brand development, these goals keep you focused on what you want to accomplish. You should not waste your time with anything included in your brand that does not strive to meet your goals.

Your "Only" Statement

Have you read the book *Zag: The Number One Strategy of High-Performance Brands* by Marty Neumeier?

It is an excellent look at how to distinguish yourself as unique in a crowded market. I had the good fortune to be taught this method at a marketing class delivered by my town's Small Business Association. The Zag method can apply to any business, and I think it's especially useful to authors as they work to understand where they fit in the market.

It will help you understand what you are bringing to your readers that is different from offerings of other authors in your genre.

Why is that important?

Understanding where you fit in the market helps you understand your brand. It can be the foundation for the brand you build for yourself.

Neumeier writes, "Customers have choices. If you don't stand out, you lose. To win, you have to answer one simple question: What makes you the 'only'?"

Take the time to do the exercise below to figure it out. I've tweaked the exercise a little bit to make it more useful for authors.

To create your "only" statement, you need to answer these six questions:

1. What genre do you write in?
2. What is the niche you write in under that genre?
3. Who are you writing for?
4. Where are you publishing?
5. What is the current trend in the genre?
6. What about your books buck that trend?

Here's an example:

I am the only romance fantasy author publishing on Amazon writing for young adults with shapeshifter characters in a market saturated with vampires.

Breaking it down, the genre is fantasy. The niche is romance. The audience is young adult. The publishing location is Amazon. The current trend is vampires. The buck of that trend is shapeshifters.

Another example:

I am the only thriller author publishing traditionally for middle-aged men writing about the Chinese mob in a market saturated with terrorist antagonists.

Can you break down the elements of that one?

Your only statement helps you define your genre, which helps you figure out where to position it on Amazon or another publishing site too. The statement also helps you define your reader, which is important when you start targeting a very specific audience with ads and social media posts.

Your goals and your only statement are the first step in building your brand. They'll keep you focused on what you're trying to accomplish. Pair those with the experience you are trying to give to a reader, and you have a strong foundation for your brand. I'll look at building that experience in the next chapter.

Wrap Up

Define your author goals. Where do you want to be in a year? How about in five, ten, or fifteen years?

Define your author business goals using the SMART method. What specifically do you want to accomplish, by when, and how will you measure it?

Determine your "only" statement. Use the Zag method to understand where you fit in the market and who your reader is.

"*A little leg work up front is always worth it for a more balanced, efficient business later on.*"

—Jenna Kutcher, *host of the #1 marketing podcast in the US: Goal Digger, The Podcast*

Nuts and Bolts

*V*isible brand is what happens after you develop the brand. Now that you know your personal author goals, your business goals, and have written your only statement, it's time to build your visible brand. Practically, you'll build those from your life and your books. Start with this: What exactly is the experience you want to provide your reader?

Keep the answer to that question in mind as you go through the steps of building your brand.

First, get to know your ideal reader. We looked at that a little bit with your only statement. I know several authors and business owners who go so far as to give their ideal reader a name and demographics. There is value in that because it will help you know where to find them online. Your marketing should be tailored to who actually reads your books and who you want to read your books (not who you *think* reads your books). You'll be able to define this person better and better over time, because you'll have analytics from social media engagement, email marketing results, and advertising responses. When you create content, talk directly to that person.

Second, define your author identity, which we did with the only statement. Your identity rests with your unique niche and how you write your books. Your genre has certain expectations. Do you know what they are? When someone picks up your book, do they know what to expect? They should. Even though the stories differ in each book, what to expect in the books and with your brand writ large should be the same.

Third, cultivate your unique author voice. Your voice, whether in your books or in marketing materials, should be distinct to you. If you are normally a soft-spoken yoga instructor, then let that be reflected in your brand. If you are normally a loud cheerleader type screaming at the TV during a football game like me, don't hide that. The more authentic your voice is to you, the easier it is to do marketing, and the more likely you'll turn fans into superfans. Remember, people buy from those they like, know, and trust. Being authentic allows that connection with the reader.

Fourth, be consistent. This is key. Once you have built yourself a framework of a brand, be consistent. All of your marketing materials (social posts, emails, ads, books, logos, covers) should consistently represent your brand, your voice, your interests—that public persona we'll develop in the next two sections.

Your public persona and the experience you offer your readers comes from your values and what you decide will be your brand. Nailing this down helps you develop content for social and emails and ads and print materials. Two ways to really figure out what you want your brand specifically to be, to sound like, to look like—to figure out what you want to share—is to mine from your life and your books.

Mine from Your Life

What do you want your readers to know about you?

Don't say "nothing" because that's not going to work. People buy from those they like, know, and trust. You, the author, are just as much a part of the brand as your books are. You have likes and dislikes, interests and hobbies. Pick two personal facts that you are willing to share with others. What part of you are you willing to share with strangers? What will keep readers interested and you comfortable?

For example, I love plant-based cooking. I don't mean that when I eat out, I just pick a salad and call it good. I mean I have been a vegetarian since I was twenty. I know every vegetarian restaurant in town and whether they are actually healthy or not. I have watched every single plant-based documentary on the internet (have you seen *The Game Changers* yet?). I am an alumni of Dr. John McDougall's 12-Day McDougall Program and the Esselstyn family's PLANTSTRONG Sedona retreat.

Everyone who knows me knows when I have a party, complete with firepits and ax throwing, the food on the table is so good, they'll never know it's plant based. One of my daughter's friends ate two bowls of chili and refused to believe me when I told her it didn't have meat in it. Even if my friends are meat eaters, they know when they show up, the food they're eating is yummy and fun, with no judgment about their own eating habits. Food is a fantastic way to bring people together.

The food is part of my brand. I'll post pics of my latest Greek Goddess salad dressing concoction, an Italian marinara casserole, or a mushroom oatmeal. My daughter and I sketched out a plant-based Southern cookbook when she was eleven, and we had a blast creating and posting.

I also love to travel. As of the writing of this book, I've been to forty-five different countries and forty-eight states. I plan to get to fifty of each before I turn fifty. I post pictures of cultural sites, beaches, mountains, jungles, locals, food, whatever I find fun and interesting about the location. Sharing the way other cultures live is really fun for me, and my followers seem to get a kick out of it.

For instance, I posted the thatched-roof farm my husband and I stayed at outside Kyoto, Japan, and the amazing food the owner's wife made for us. In the Philippines, I learned how to use an underwater camera, which is super cool in those incredible clear blue waters.

For my day job, I get to spend a lot of time in Germany. So I routinely post pretzels, baked goods, traditional bands playing randomly on the walkplatz, river paths, castle ruins, and cuckoo clocks. The walkplatzs are my favorite places to hang out. They are like city centers with no cars. Tons of restaurants, pubs, churches, museums, and festivals—they are great places to people watch or just pass the time.

A word on privacy and security for travel posts. I don't post my itinerary, ever. I normally don't post while I'm traveling either unless I'm gone for a significant period of time. One year, we were in Costa Rica for two weeks, and I turned off every electronic device I owned. I took a stand-alone camera instead of using my phone, and rather than posting pictures in real time, I waited until I got home and posted every day for two weeks. That can actually be fun when people think I'm still gone.

When I'm on vacation, I want to stay on vacation. I don't want to worry about security or marketing. So I relax and don't worry about marketing. Before I leave, I plan out my regular social media posts and use a scheduler like Later or Hootsuite so I can just relax on vacation, and my marketing still chugs right along.

The point is that we don't need social media to invade every part of our lives. We control what we put out and when. What I post is innocuous—food and travel—but it's something I'm known for, and people enjoy. I do not talk about my day job much because that could cause too many problems, and I don't post about my family much, either, to protect their privacy.

I don't want you to feel compelled to share every single part of your life or to be turned off because you feel you need to.

You don't. You get to decide what you share. You get to decide what your brand will be. If sharing something makes you uncomfortable, then do not make that part of your public persona.

But authors use this tactic all the time. Romance author Kristy Woodson Harvey is also a home decorator and her before-and-after shots of gorgeous homes in North Carolina are a great insight into her other interests. Steampunk author Gail Carriger is an archaeologist. Can you imagine the cool things she posts? I know other authors who decide to become television show experts. Do you have a favorite television show? Become an expert on it and post regularly.

Building your brand also includes your books. Now that you have a couple of personal interests you can be known for, let's look at your books.

Mine from Your Books

Your books or stories are a gold mine. You can dig in them for ideas. As you look through your books, keep in mind that whatever you choose to make part of your brand, you better enjoy it. If you don't, that will show through in your products. Make sure whatever you choose is something you can really become an expert on and have fun posting about consistently.

To start, go through your main character, minor characters, and antagonist.

- What are their jobs?
- What are their hobbies?
- What do they hate? Love?
- What activities are in their daily habits?
- Do they own pets? Have kids? Take care of parents?

Think about your setting:

- Where is it?

- What is the culture of the town, city, country?
- What foods do they eat?
- What activities are prevalent in the place?

Now, what about the themes and messages:

- Love conquers all?
- Big city versus small-town life?
- Family first?
- Good guys always win?
- CIA black ops guys with unique skills?

All of the answers give you room to play with your posts because you are introducing your characters and your books to your followers, whether it's a book in progress or one already published. You can use this material to create a community online for readers.

If you're a nonfiction author, think about what you're trying to teach someone with your book:

- Define the problem or question you're solving in your book.
- Develop the reasons why the problem/question exists.
- Create a list of possible solutions.
- Brainstorm a list of why you are the expert to help readers solve this problem or answer the question.
- Explain how the solutions work.
- Explain what the reader must do to implement the solutions.

This technique works for anyone writing a nonfiction book, because they are teaching a reader something. Once you figure out what that is, you've basically defined the intent. Your questions will almost always be how or why:

- Who are the greatest football coaches of all time and why?

- How do I install a security system?
- What were the causes of WWI?
- Is the food industry to blame for America's obesity epidemic?
- How do satellites drive the modern way of life?
- What are the best websites for travel deals?

For memoir, you can use what works from the fiction side, since you are telling a story. You can also use what works from the nonfiction side, especially if there's a moral or theme in the book you want to leave the reader with.

Putting It All Together

Once you figure out what you can use from your books to build your brand, you need to ask yourself if the three to five points you've chosen reflect the values and promises you want to make to your readers.

Look at your list. You should have these elements:

- Your personal author goal
- Your business goals as an author
- Your only statement
- Your ideal reader
- The values, promises—the experience—you offer your reader
- Two to three personal facts you want to be known for
- Two to three items of interest from your books you can add to your brand
- This list is your full brand. The next chapter will explain what you do with it.

Wrap up

Define your reader. Before you create a single piece of content, understand who you are talking to. Who is reading your work? Talk directly to that person for the most effective marketing.
Define your author identity and unique voice. Your "only" statement is foundational to understanding your identity and where you fit in the market. The tone you use should reflect your identity. Use it consistently.

Mine from your life and your books. To help you build marketing content and to better define your brand, look to your own interests and the characteristics of the characters in your books.

"In order to be irreplaceable, one must always be different."

—Coco Chanel, founder of Chanel

What Do I Do with My Brand?

*W*hat now? Now that you have a solid brand, what do you do with it? This chapter will get into the nitty-gritty of expanding that brand into a usable marketing tool. The foundation of your brand was developed with your goals, your public persona, your "only" statement, and the values and experience you want to bring to the reader. Taking all of that, let's develop your author bio and the visual aspects of your brand that should attract readers—logo, fonts, color, word choice.

Author Bios

A strong author bio introduces an author to the reader. It establishes your credibility, likability, and relevance. You'll use it in a variety of ways. You'll want a long version and a short version. The short version should be roughly 100 to 200 words.

What Do I Do with My Brand?

This version is used for book jacket blurbs, Amazon author bios, conference bios, and media kits.

The longer version can be anywhere from 250 to 400 words. You'll want to use this version on your website, and if an organizer needs more information. Write it in third person (about you, not by you). Even if you write children's books, third person is more professional and says you are taking your career seriously.

To create the meat of your bio, include these elements:

Your name. Whether it's a pen name or your real name, it seems obvious, but your name needs to be on your bio.

Only statement. Consider including your only statement to tell the reader specifically what you're writing and how it's different.

Reader experience. Tell the reader exactly what experience they will get reading your work or hanging out in your world.

Credentials. Any degrees, awards, or recognitions that pertain to your work add credibility. Also include affiliations with relevant organizations.

Notable works. This can include best-sellers or popular titles or publications with notable outlets.

Personal touch. Any interesting anecdotes you want to share. Use what you mined from your life here.

Call to action. At the bottom of the bio, tell them what you want them to do. People don't have time to infer. So whether it's signing up for email, registering with your writers' group, or buying a book, be explicit.

Here's an example of a good bio from author Lucy Score.

> Lucy Score is an instant #1 New York Times bestselling author. She grew up in a literary family who insisted that the dinner table was for reading and earned a degree in

journalism. She writes full-time from the Pennsylvania home she and Mr. Lucy share with their obnoxious cat, Cleo. When not spending hours crafting heartbreaker heroes and kick-ass heroines, Lucy can be found on the couch, in the kitchen, or at the gym. She hopes to someday write from a sailboat, oceanfront condo, or tropical island with reliable Wi-Fi. Sign up for her never annoying newsletter at: https://www.lucyscore.net/subscribe-lucys-newsletter-website/

Number of words: *99*

Name: *Lucy Score*

Reader experience: *"heartbreaker heroes" "kick-ass heroines"*

Credentials: *instant #1 New York Times best-seller, journalism degree*

Personal touch: *She grew up in a literary family. Lucy can be found on the couch, in the kitchen, or at the gym. She hopes to someday write from a sailboat, oceanfront condo, or tropical island with reliable Wi-Fi.*

Call to action*: sign up for her newsletter*

My thoughts: Although she's missing notable works, her only statement, her #1 NYT best-seller credential, is enough to entice a reader to look for more. I do think she could use some of the "personal" space to tell the reader about her series, but she is a best-seller, so the bio works for her, and I won't quibble.

Here's another example from one of my favorite thriller authors, C. J. Box:

C. J. Box is the #1 New York Times *best-selling author of thirty novels including the Joe Pickett series. He won the Edgar Alan Poe Award for Best Mystery Novel (*Blue Heaven, *2008) as well as the Anthony Award, Prix Calibre 38 (France), the Maltese Falcon Award (Japan), the Macavity Award, the Gumshoe Award, two Barry Awards,* *and the 2010 Mountains & Plains Independent Booksellers Association Award for fiction. He was recently awarded the 2016 Western Heritage Award for Literature by the National Cowboy Museum as well as the Spur Award for Best Contemporary Novel by the Western Writers of America in 2017. Over 10 million copies of his books have been sold in the US and abroad and they've been translated into twenty-seven languages. Two television series based on his novels are in production (*BIG SKY *on ABC and* JOE PICKETT *on Spectrum Originals and Paramount+). He is an Executive Producer for both series.*

Shadows Reel, *the twenty-second Joe Pickett novel, was published in March of 2021 and debuted at #2 on the* New York Times *best-seller list and #1 on the* Wall Street Journal *best-seller list.*

Box is a Wyoming native and has worked as a ranch hand, surveyor, fishing guide, a small-town newspaper reporter and editor, and he owned an international tourism marketing firm with his wife, Laurie. In 2008, Box was awarded the "BIG WYO" Award from the state tourism industry. An avid outdoorsman, Box has hunted, fished, hiked, ridden, and skied throughout Wyoming and the Mountain West. He served on the Board of Directors for the Cheyenne Frontier Days Rodeo and currently serves on the Wyoming Office of Tourism Board. They have three daughters and two grandchildren. He and his wife, Laurie, live on their ranch in Wyoming.

Number of words: *293*

Name: *C. J. Box*

Reader experience: *This is a bit subtle, but his list of awards tells you you're reading mystery and the fact that his books have sold over 10 million copies tells you they are a well-loved series. His personal anecdotes about his hobbies are a good indication of what you'll find in his work too—rugged outdoorsman who likes hunting and fishing in the Mountain West.*

Credentials: *small-town reporter/editor; owned a marketing firm; winner of Edgar Alan Poe Award and many others*

Personal touch: *An avid outdoorsman, Box has hunted, fished, hiked, ridden, and skied throughout Wyoming and the Mountain West. He served on the Board of Directors for the Cheyenne Frontier Days Rodeo and currently serves on the Wyoming Office of Tourism Board. They have three daughters and two grandchildren. He and his wife, Laurie, live on their ranch in Wyoming.*

Call to action: *Two television series based on his novels are in production on Spectrum and Paramount.*

My thoughts: It's a bit wordy. At his level, being a *New York Times* best-seller, he doesn't need to list all the awards anymore. I like his personal anecdotes because we know this is an outdoorsman. I would have liked to see two things: a stronger call to action, and a stronger tie to his books. A small tweak would be to tell readers explicitly to check out the series on Spectrum or Paramount but that's quibbling a bit. And because I read his books religiously, I know his personal anecdotes are a direct correlation to what he writes about. But a new reader may not. It's subtle but readers only give you about three seconds. Otherwise, this bio hits all the main points. I mean, I'm always going to read everything he writes anyway.

One more example from steamy romance author and a friend of mine, Robin Covington:

A **USA Today** *and* **Wall Street Journal** *best-seller, Robin Covington loves to explore the theme of fooling around and falling in love in her books. Her stories burn up the sheets . . . one page at a time. A biracial author of Native American descent, Robin proudly writes diverse romance where everyone gets their happy ever after.*

She is an unapologetic Indiginerd and comic book geek. She hoards red nail polish and stalks Chris Evans.

A 2016 RITA® Award finalist, Robin's books have won the National Reader's Choice and Golden Leaf Awards and finaled in the Romantic Times Reviewer's Choice, HOLT Medallion, and the Book Seller's Best.

She lives in Maryland with her handsome husband, her two brilliant children (they get it from her, of course!), and her beloved furbaby, Dixie Joan Wilder (Yes—THE Joan Wilder).

Drop her a line at robin@robincovingtonromance.com—she always writes back.

Number of words: 143

Name: *Robin Covington*

Reader experience: *fooling around and falling in love; diverse romance where everyone gets their happy ever after*

Credentials. USA Today *and* Wall Street Journal *best-seller; RITA finalist and other awards*

Personal touch. *Her beloved furbaby Dixie Joan Wilder*

Call to action. *Drop her a line at robin@robincovingtonromance.com—she always writes back.*

My thoughts: This is a good length and easy to read. She doesn't include an only statement but, honestly, not many authors use that technique. However, it can be inferred with the last sentence of the first paragraph: *A biracial author of Native American descent, Robin proudly writes diverse romance where everyone gets their happy ever after.* I would encourage Robin to be more direct with her call to action. Maybe direct readers to sign up for her newsletter or follow her on social rather than email. Otherwise, I just love the name of her dog and this is a pretty solid bio.

Logos

Logos are more for hybrid and indie authors than traditional authors but I still encourage traditionally published authors to work with their publicist on one. They are a vital component to any business identity. They should reflect your goals, your values, and the experience you offer the reader. Your logo can leave a lasting impression on a reader.

To develop your logo, you can use a marketing company or do it yourself. If you're doing it yourself online, then I recommend Canva or Tailor Brands and keep the following in mind:

Keep it simple. A strong logo should be simple and easy to recognize.

Memorable. Brand recognition is important and if a reader knows your logo, they'll immediately stop and check out your book.

Relevant. If you write horror and your logo is a red heart, that's a mismatch in relevance. Make sure your logo is relevant to the experience.

Timeless. You're going to be stuck with this logo for most of your career. Make sure you like it and make sure it is not tied to a specific trend, so it won't be quickly outdated.

Versatile. Your logo needs to work on a variety of platforms, on and off line—website, social media, bookmarks, brochures, book covers. It needs to work in color and in black and white, and in various sizes.

Unique. Make sure your logo stands out and does not look like other logos. To do that, avoid clichés so you don't dilute your own brand.

Colors. Yes, colors matter. If you are writing billionaire romances, red and black can work. But light pink or purple won't. Different colors can evoke different emotions, so think about that as you're choosing. The London Image Institute has a great list that I've taken a few liberties with: red=excitement, strength, sex; orange=confidence, success, sociable; yellow=creativity, happiness, warmth; green=healing, freshness, quality; blue=trust, peace, loyalty; pink=compassion, sincerity, innocence; purple=luxury, spirituality; brown=rugged, simple, dependable; black=formal, dramatic, power; white=clean, simplicity, innocence.

You might consider testing your logo with your audience. Throw out two or three ideas to your email list or Instagram followers or Facebook group and see what they think. The logo really isn't for you. It's for your readers, so what you might think is excellent may not do it for them.

Same with book covers, right? You may love your design, but we as writers can get too close and attached to elements such as logos and covers. But our readers don't really have that emotional attachment to them and can help us really think through what is resonating with them. So I recommend you give that a try.

Fonts, Imagery, and Tone

Believe it or not, font matters. Fonts say something, and you want to make sure they are saying the correct message about your brand. I'm not talking about font for the interior of your book. This kind of font is for marketing purposes only, and the font you choose for your printed marketing products and digital posts should align with the values and experience you bring to the reader. A playful font might be great for a rom-com or a children's book, but for a horror or thriller? Not so much.

Choose a font that evokes the kind of emotion your brand should evoke. Serif fonts can feel traditional and formal. Sans-serif are considered modern and clean. Scripts tend to be more elegant or creative. Regardless of which you choose, make sure it conveys the message you intend to convey with your marketing.

Make sure the font you choose is legible and easy to read. If your font is difficult to read, potential readers will bolt to somewhere else. Test your fonts with your readership or trusted partners. Make sure they are easy to read from a distance as well because we want to make it as easy as possible for our readers to get the point no matter where they see that font.

Fonts are a critical element of your brand because they can influence how your readers perceive the brand. Font impacts readability and attention. Thoughtful font selection is essential to resonating with your readers, so choose wisely and be consistent in your application of that font.

Photography is also just as essential. What photos are you using on your website, your social, your print materials? If they look amateurish, then your reader will think you're amateurish. Don't smartphone your official bio pic. Have a professional take that shot.

For social stories and posts, smartphone cameras are fine, but bear in mind what story those photos are saying, and that includes the quality of the photo. If it's a casual outing with friends or a book signing, then phone camera photos are fine. If it's for marketing materials for a conference or a media kit, you're going to want quality, professional photos.

As you think through the type of photos and video you want to use on your website, social, and print materials, think through the purpose of the imagery.

Videos are king on the internet. Photos are queen. Visual appeal matters because humans are inherently visual beings. Good quality, compelling images can grab the attention of a reader or potential reader and create a lasting impression. A good photo or video can convey a very specific message, evoke emotions, and tell a story more effectively than text alone. Writers are inherently storytellers. Photos are just a different medium for that story. So think about the story the photo or video and the quality of those is telling before you post them.

Imagery is really important to establishing your brand. Consistent use of styles of photos can help consumers recognize and remember you and your books, which can significantly influence whether a reader will buy your books or not.

Imagery can also tell a reader how serious you take your career. If you are presenting yourself and your books in the best possible light, then that alone can instill confidence in readers and potential readers. The power of imagery cannot be overstated. In the saturated market we work in, you have about three seconds to grab a reader's attention. Does your photo or video do that?

For social media alone, you are trying to break through someone's mindless scrolling. You really have about three seconds to do that. Put the point up front. It's like backstory in fiction or foundational history in nonfiction; no one wants to read it until they've been hooked on the book. Have you done that with your imagery right up front?

Some best practices for using that three seconds to hook your reader:

Make sure to use on-screen text for photos, and captions for video. More than 69 percent of video is watched without sound, so to reach a reader, use text too.

Give the viewer the benefit right up front. Not what your book is about but what they'll get out of it. Will it entertain them? How? Will it inform or educate them? On what? Make that clear immediately.

A picture is worth a thousand words, right? Well what words does your photo tell? If you aren't sure, go back to the drawing board. Yes, in some cases, our book covers will be the visual. But in other cases, a good quality photo can tell the story without the cover. It can also depict an exciting event for the reader (book signing, anyone?).

If you're producing a video for Reels or Stories or YouTube, the music can be a key tool to grab a reader's attention. Even explainer videos have music. That's because music can also evoke an emotion. What emotion do you want your reader to feel when they scroll through your content? Use music to help.

The bottom line with font and imagery is that you are telling a story. You are just doing it with your font and your imagery. If you think about it that way, it should be easier to do. You, after all, are a storyteller.

Finally, the tone and word choice you use are equally important. They are not just superficial aspects of your brand. They are as fundamental as your bio and your logo and your values. They build your brand identity and help you connect with your audience. If you want to build an effective, creative, and impactful brand, you need to pay attention to the tone of your materials and the words you choose to use.

Tone reflects your values and the experience you are offering the reader. The tone and word choice you decide on should resonate with your ideal reader. Use language that speaks directly to your reader so you can foster a deep connection that can turn a curious reader into a fan and then into a superfan.

This applies to every aspect of your marketing. If you are posting about a summer vacation to the Grand Canyon with your family and you write hometown, closed-door romances but use a tone of disparagement of all the tourists and the heat and the cost, that probably doesn't resonate with your brand. I know we all have off days, but on those days, play it safe and maybe don't post at all. On the other hand, if you write raunchy, bawdy characters and have an established brand using profanity, then use it even talking about a family summer vacation.

That being said, unless you're building a brand of a complaining curmudgeon, I recommend saving the complaining for offline. You are trying to build a community of readers who resonate with your work, who want to buy from you, who want to be part of your life. Most of the time, that does not include a bunch of complaining.

Does that mean you have to be inspirational, perky, and uplifting all the time? No. Unless of course that's your brand. But it does mean that studies have shown us most people are put off by complaining, politics, and religion. So I'd stay away from those subjects.

I think the easiest way to think about this is genre. Would you offer sweet, soft language for a horror or thriller? Probably not. What about using profanity for a sweet, small-town romance? Nope. Think through what experience you want to offer a reader, and choose fonts, imagery, tone, and words that reflect that. If you aren't sure, email me or test it out with your writer buddies. No book gets out without a tribe, so take advantage of the writing community you have. If you don't have one, Pikes Peak Writers in Colorado Springs is my favorite conference. All genres, all level of writers. Join us anytime.

Wrap Up

Author bio. Whether short or long, use the elements listed to help you. Credentials, reader experience and your only statement are strong aspects of a good author bio. The fun anecdote about you makes it personal and gives the reader something to identify with.

Logo. Your logo says everything about your brand in one image. Make sure it reflects the experience you want to bring to the reader. Use it everywhere and consistently.

Font, imagery, and tone. While font, imagery, tone, and word choice seem like peripheral elements of your brand, they are actually the visual representation of your brand. So take time to ensure they are evoking the emotion you want to evoke in your reader.

"Repetition makes reputation, and reputation makes customers."

—Elizabeth Arden, founder of Elizabeth Arden Inc.

5.

Market Your Brand

*D*eveloping your brand is the first step. At its very foundation, your brand is the experience you want to offer a reader. Once you know that, you can develop your bio and all the visuals that go along with that. Now, we'll take all those elements and create content you can use to market your brand.

Do you like creating? Since you're an author, I assume you do. And because you like creating, you're in luck. Photos, videos, blogs, podcasts, social posts, emails, and ads are all types of content you can create from the foundational elements of your brand.

Compelling content comes from understanding what makes people tick. You already know that readers buy from people they like, know, and trust. How do you get them to like, know, and trust you?

You need to make them cry. Or laugh. Or fall in love or scare them to death. For nonfiction, make them wonder and delight and hope at your information. Turn on a lightbulb. For both types of writing, hit them with a two-by-four of emotional compelling content. Give them all the feels you can manage.

Content is key in your online presence. There are two ways to think about content marketing. One is to use content to drive traffic to your website. This can be social media posts or emails. Another way is a bit more complicated. Blogs, podcasts, websites with tons and tons of content so search engines will send potential readers to your site is an advanced form of content marketing. Blogging and podcasting are excellent marketing techniques, but they require a lot of time and energy. These are advanced forms of marketing your brand that require knowledge of search engine optimization. You decide if that's you or not.

No matter if you are creating content on social or in emails or for your blogs and podcasts, your content needs to meet one of these three objectives: educate, inform, or entertain. Posts that educate, inform, or entertain should also accomplish one of three results: reinforce a belief, refute an argument, or renew a discussion. This formula is how you get readers to feel and to think. The content you create, to include the tone and fonts you use, allows the reader to get to know you, and that's the goal—an authentic experience with the author either through content or your books.

Create Compelling Content

Let's break down the three objectives of content marketing.

The first type of objective is to **educate** your followers on something you really enjoy doing. Think back to your brand. What are your hobbies and those of your characters? Hiking, fishing, cross-stitching, pottery? Fun activities that you enjoy is something you can educate your community about.

Let's look at how your educational posts can meet the three results:

- Reinforce what people already know: Only grandpas fly-fish anymore (kidding). Hiking in the mountains will get you killed because of bears (also kidding).
- Refute an argument: Grandpas aren't the only ones who fly-fish. Hiking trails are all groomed and available for every level hiker.
- Renew a discussion: Why you should take up fly fishing. Why the Appalachian Trail should be rerouted.

The second type of objective is to **inform**. This sort of post discusses an event you want to let people know about. Are you attending a retreat, conference, or workshop? Do you have a speaking gig somewhere? What are you doing? More importantly, what's the progress of your book? Those are also inform-type posts.

- Reinforce the dates and locations.
- Refute someone who got something wrong. I call this one "correcting the record" politely so you don't sound like a jerk.
- Renew a discussion about the event. Who's going? What are they looking forward to? What will they ask the speaker?

Finally, a post that **entertains** is just that, entertaining—the third type of objective. Charles Dickens said, "There is nothing in the world so irresistibly contagious as laughter and good humor."

Make your posts something fun. Tell jokes. Deliver games or trivia. Share hilarious videos. Pull out fun activities going on with your community or in your life. I know it sounds funny that you can reinforce, refute, or renew a post meant to entertain, but you can.

- Reinforce a belief: Hot air ballooning is awesome. Post a video.

- Refute an argument: Salsarita's is better than Chipotle. Period.
- Renew a discussion: What is the best streaming series right now?

I want to emphasize one point when you are thinking about what you are posting and why. Opinions, your opinions, matter. Remember your brand? This is where you utilize that brand. People engage because they have an emotional reaction to something you said. That is not to say you need to weigh in on politics or religion. In today's world, I wouldn't unless you are selling books in a political niche and that's part of your brand.

But here's the interesting thing: if you don't have opinions on anything, then your posts are boring and vanilla, and people will go elsewhere. If you're just parroting what everyone else is saying, then you aren't providing worthy content. You want to give an opinion to evoke emotion because then followers will talk. If you can get people talking, that is gold.

Opinions on topics such as television shows, sports, outdoor hobbies, crafts, and the like make it a fun discussion instead of a heated debate. A fun and interesting discussion is what you want. Heated debates are fine depending on the topic, but alienating potential readers is not fine. And that's the goal. Increasing your readership.

Web Presence

In today's online world, having a web presence or digital footprint is no longer an option. Did you know 79 percent of shoppers shop online at least once a month? Online shopping has simply become a part of modern life. Nearly 97 million people shop on social media with millennials shopping on social media the most.

Books are sold online—77 percent of readers buy their books from Amazon and that is both in print, ebook, and audiobook versions. But even in brick-and-mortar stores, consumers use their smartphones to look up prices and buy. Have you ever been in a Barnes & Noble and looked up the same book on Amazon? I know I have.

My point is that shopping has increasingly moved online, and authors need to take advantage of that. In this section, I'll focus on websites and how to ensure your website reflects your brand because the same principles apply to your social media. If you plan to sell books, then you need an author website. That's not necessarily true of social media.

A quick word on social. Plenty of authors sell books using online strategies without using social media. That's not to say you shouldn't be on social. Instagram, Facebook, TikTok, Pinterest, and YouTube are all great places to build and sustain your reader community. You can increase email marketing lists, which is the gold standard for selling books (ads is next). But do you absolutely need social media to sell books and build an author brand? Not really. That cannot be said of a website.

In this day and age, authors simply can't afford not to have a website. The majority of your readers will visit your website before they buy your book. What happens if they Google you and you aren't there? The first impression won't be very good. With a website, you're telling your readers you take your career seriously and it builds your legitimacy as a small business.

When you build that site, it can't be one you slap together and call it good. You don't have to pay thousands for someone to build it for you either. WordPress, Wix, Weebly, HubSpot, Gator, and others offer free templates that are relatively easy to set up.

But before we get into the actual website, let's ask *when* you need a website? I ask this of all authors. When do you need a website? When do you need social media? An email list?

The answer is this: Not until you have products to sell, period. If you have not completed your books, you have no business marketing them. Concentrate on creating products. Then, concentrate on building your marketing plan, which includes developing your brand.

Some authors find marketing their work before it's done a solid marketing strategy. If it motivates you to finish your work, or if you are an established author with a pre-order deadline, then I say go for it. But if you are new, and have not finished your book yet, I am on the side of this argument that says finish the book first. I've seen too many authors focus on the marketing instead of the book and years go by before they complete them.

Let's say you have products to sell and you're ready to go. What do you do with your website? You create a space for readers to learn about you, sign up for your email, and buy your books. At its very core, that's it. That's all your website needs. Your bio, a call to action, and links to buy your books.

I get asked a lot if having a website means authors have to blog. That question gets into the purpose of your website. Starting out, your website is a calling card, a business card, for your business. Content marketing, which is what blogging and podcasting are, is a much more long-term marketing strategy. Regular posts are a great tool for any author who has the time and energy to invest in search engine optimization and daily writing on something outside of their books.

If that's you, then go for it. If you're interested in content marketing but don't want to blog, one way to do it is to post industry news. The more information your website has, the more search engines have to index. That indexed information makes it easier for search engines like Google to show your website in a search about books in your genre. If you decide to create content in the form of a blog or a podcast or a news repository, create content for both web and social using the 30-50-20 rule.

This rule says that 30% of your posts should be original content. This is the information about your and your books and where to buy them. The next 50% of your content should be curated. That means posting interesting information that comes from your brand. So if part of your brand is providing a spy thriller adventure, then scan various global spy organizations websites for interesting news and post. Finally, the last 20% of your content should be fun and engaging: humorous memes or videos, polls, trivia, things your reader can respond to.

But at its fundamental purpose, an author website is a tool to give information to readers. Use your logo, font, tone, and word choice the same. Be consistent with your brand across all your web platforms.

If you are just using your website as a tool for information, that's totally fine. Your website serves as an online home for your readers. It's a place where readers can find information about you and your books all the time, no matter their time zone, which opens up a global market for you. Did you know Germany is the third largest market for books in the world?

Your website is simply a visual tool that represents your brand and the experience you're offering your readers. A well-designed and professional website can enhance your credibility, likability, and trustworthiness, because (say it with me) people buy from those they like, know, and trust.

Another reason to have a website is you can also sell directly to readers on it. Doing that gives you valuable customer data to help you focus your marketing. You can run online advertising campaigns, collect feedback, and promote your books with your website. This gets into a little bit of market analysis and data. Once you start selling books, that information is invaluable.

Last, your website is a good place to store your media kit. When you speak at a conference or give an author talk or do a book signing, a media kit makes it super easy on the event organizers. You can email the organizers the link to your website's media kit page, and an ebook copy of your book. Your media kit should include a long and short bio and a professional high-resolution and low-resolution photo. You can also include a "where to buy my book" sheet with a QR code on it. Something else to consider is an updated press release that includes your most recent title, a prewritten introduction for an emcee, Qs and As for an interviewer, and links to other media appearances. This includes radio, television, podcasts, webinars and really anytime you've been featured anywhere. An example of a press release is in the bonus section.

Could you use social media outlets like Facebook, Instagram, or TikTok to do the same thing as your website? Of course you can, but you don't own those outlets. You build a website; then you own it and its content. It can exist as an information hub for your readers. You can showcase your writing portfolio, event schedule, and any offers you're making. It is your home, your information hub, your repository online. Using social media for those purposes risks the whims of the social outlet. It also risks your professional credibility because websites have simply become an expectation of consumers, to include readers.

Print Products

Have you heard the term *swag* or *merch*? These are just fun terms for merchandise related to your book. They are a type of brand marketing you can use for a variety of purposes. Types of swag or merch vary. Printed paper products are items such as bookmarks, posters, door hangers, postcards, notepads, and even trading cards (those are fun for series authors with a lot of characters).

Non-paper merch includes buttons, mugs, stickers, pens, coins. I got a tiny little sewing kit from Susan Wiggs as swag when she gave an author talk at my book club on her book *The Oysterville Sewing Circle*. How clever, right?

Oriental Trading Company and VistaPrint are two great sites to browse for ideas for your swag. Just keep in mind, the brand principle applies. Be consistent with your tone, logo, font, and colors.

Do you absolutely need printed products? No. It's like good food at a Super Bowl party. Your friends will remember that they had a great time at the party. If you serve great food, that's just a bonus. Think of swag as a cherry on top of brand marketing. Yummy but not totally necessary.

If you are going to utilize printed products for your brand, consider the following elements to help you create compelling and memorable swag:

- **Determine the purpose of the swag.** If you want to just increase the experience a reader has with you, give it away for free. If you are looking to increase your email distro list, then give it away in exchange (sign up for my email list and I will send you x).
- **Know your ideal reader.** What type of swag would your reader expect? If you're writing Westerns, would your readers like or expect a heart-shaped lollipop? Probably not. But a belt buckle with your logo? Darn tootin'!
- **Budget and quality.** Be careful buying cheap merchandise. That can send just as strong a message as good quality swag.
- **Design.** With everything else, be consistent. Use your logo, font, tone, and word choice the same with every piece of branding you use for marketing.
- **Consider useful.** How much swag have you thrown out? I always use the bookmarks and pens and water bottles. But the keychains? Not so much. So consider how useful your swag can be to a reader. The more useful, the better.

The key to good swag is that it provides value to your reader while, at the same time, effectively marketing your brand and promoting the experience you are offering. Quality, relevance, and creativity are essential to achieve that goal.

Where do you give swag out? Everywhere. Really. If you're doing a formal author event, talk, or signing, have it on the table for your reader. But if you're going to a writers conference, readers conference, book club, school event, have it on hand. You can also have it for your superfans. If you have digital swag, that's super easy for delivery to your superfans.

Wrap Up

Compelling content. You are trying to evoke an emotion and an action, whether that's sign up for your newsletter, follow you on social, or buy your book. Use the rule of thirds to create good content online.

Web presence. Your website is your online calling card. Create it professionally and with intention. A basic site includes a bio, a photo of you, the book cover, and where to buy your books. More advanced authors can use content marketing to increase the site's search engine optimization.

Print products. People like free things. When you attend an event, a conference, a book signing, or an author talk, take printed products with you. Even if it's a bookmark, it's not just a free item, it's a calling card for your brand.

Bonus Material

*B*uilding a strong, identifiable, effective brand takes time. Spend some time and effort developing yours. The benefits to your career are priceless. In the saturated literary market we are all working in, having a solid brand not only helps your readers connect with you and remember you, but it also makes your marketing a little bit easier.

Your brand gives you a framework, a box, your right and left limits, for where to direct your energy. This bonus section gives you a checklist to help you create your brand. I encourage you to read the entire book first to put into context the steps the checklist directs you to do. I wish you tons of luck and good fortune on your author career and your writing journey. Feel free to reach out anytime.

Bonus #1: Your Author Brand Checklist

(Use this as a guide to planning out your author brand)

Determine your personal author goals
- Where do you want to be in 5, 10, 20 years?

Determine your author business goals
- Monthly, annual income
- Books produced and published
- Marketing tactics

Identify your ideal reader
- Demographics
- Likes/dislikes
- Why they read your genre

Develop your public persona
- Only statement
- Hobbies
- Tone/language
- Experience you want to provide your reader

Write your bio
- Your name
- Only statement
- Reader experience
- Credentials
- Notable works

- Personal touch
- Call to action

Design your logo and visual brand
- Keep it simple
- Memorable
- Relevant and timeless
- Versatile
- Unique
- Colors that match your brand

Create your website
- Bio
- Books
- Sign up

Create a press kit
- Bio
- High – and low-res photos
- Web and social addresses

Design your print materials
- Logo
- Fonts
- Colors
- Tone
- Word choice

Bonus #2: Author Press Release Example

Mustard Couch Press
2308 Mt Vernon Ave #440
Alexandria, VA 22301
123-456-7890

January 1, 2024

FOR IMMEDIATE RELEASE

ALEXANDRIA, Va.—Mustard Couch Press today announced the latest work from marketing expert Jenny Kate, *Branding for Authors: Creating an Author Brand for Busy Writers*, to hit Amazon January 1.

Branding for Authors is an informative how-to focused on helping authors build a business brand from scratch. Jenny Kate details all the elements of a strong author brand and gives advice on how to use it to grow an author business and sell books. This easy-to-read and easy-to-implement guide will help authors at any level of their careers build a strong, effective author brand.

Jenny Kate has been a communicator, marketer, and teacher since 2001. She co-founded Writer Nation to help authors become authorpreneurs. She holds a master's degree in English, is the Director of the Pikes Peak Writers Conference, and sat on the board of Washington Romance Writers for five years. Her book, *Social Media for Authors*, hit #4 on Amazon best-seller's list.

For more information, contact Jenny Kate at writernationjen@gmail.com or visit www.thewriternation.com

###

Acknowledgments

No book comes into the world without a tribe of people to get it there. I want to thank Pikes Peak Writers, Washington Romance Writers, all members of the Writer Nation Facebook Group, and every writer I've ever met for being my tribe.

Abigail Riccardi, my virtual assistant and sanity check. Sandra Wendel, my amazing editor who knows how to tell me when my stuff sucks and when it doesn't. Miss Thing who has been with me since the beginning. My husband who supports me all the time, even when I blow off the International Balloon Fiesta to meet a deadline.

About the Author

Jenny Kate has been a communicator, marketer, teacher, and public relations professional since 2001. She holds a master's degree in English, and was Director of the Pikes Peak Writers Conference in 2022, 2023, and 2024. She blogs for Pikes Peak Writers, judges contests for the Utah League of Writers, and was on the board of Washington Romance Writers for five years.

With her husband, Jenny Kate co-founded Writer Nation, an online community for writers to learn effective marketing and sell more books. She issues a monthly newsletter with tips, advice, news, and information. She is also the host of the Writer Nation Podcast where she chats with writers and industry professionals.

A born Alabama girl, she bleeds crimson and white. When she isn't writing or teaching about marketing, she travels the world looking for the world's best vegan sandwich. So far, tofu banh

About the Author

mi in Hoi An, Vietnam, is winning that race.

Check out her current books:

Social Media for Authors: Book Marketing for Writers Who'd Rather Write

Social Media for Authors Workbook

Advertising for Authors: Advertising Basics for Writers Who'd Rather Write

Instagram for Authors: A Quick Primer for Busy Writers

Feel free to reach out to her anytime with marketing or publishing questions:

Web: www.thewriternation.com

Instagram: @writernationjen

Facebook.com/groups/WriterNation

Email: writernationjen@gmail.com

Made in the USA
Middletown, DE
07 March 2024

50983626R00040